How to Analyze People Effectively:

Learn to Read People's Intentions at Work & In Relationships through Body Language to Boost your People Skills & Achieve Success

Steve Chambers

© Copyright 2018 by Steve Chambers - All rights reserved.

The contents of this book may not be reproduced, duplicated or transmitted without direct written permission from the author.

Under no circumstances will any legal responsibility or blame be held against the publisher for any reparation, damages, or monetary loss due to the information herein, either directly or indirectly.

Legal Notice:

This book is copyright protected. This is only for personal use. You cannot amend, distribute, sell, use, quote or paraphrase any part or the content within this book without the consent of the author.

Disclaimer Notice:

Please note the information contained within this document is for educational and entertainment purposes only. Every attempt has been made to provide accurate, up to date and reliable complete information. No warranties of any kind are expressed or implied. Readers acknowledge that the author is not engaging in the rendering of legal, financial, medical or professional advice. The content of this book has been derived from various sources. Please consult a licensed professional before attempting any techniques outlined in this book.

By reading this document, the reader agrees that under no circumstances are is the author responsible for any losses, direct or indirect, which are incurred as a result of the use of information contained within this document, including, but not limited to, —errors, omissions, or inaccuracies.

Table of Contents

Introduction:

Chapter 1: How to Analyze People Effectively: Getting Started

Chapter 2: Analyzing Human Behavior

Chapter 3: Evaluating the Different Personality Types

Chapter 4: How to Analyze People Quickly

Chapter 5: Reading Someone's Mind like a Pro

Chapter 6: Reading People through Facial Expressions

Chapter 7: Analyzing People through the Words they Say

Chapter 8: Analyzing Someone on Dating Situations

Chapter 9: How to Detect if Someone is Lying or Trying to Deceive You

Chapter 10: Detecting Danger Before it is Too Late

Conclusion

What This Book Will Teach You

Are you curious to learn how to read people's intentions better through their nonverbal cues in order to respond effectively and succeed in your career and relationships?

Have you always wanted to know more about human behavior and to boost your people skills in order to get ahead in your career?

If these questions relate well with you, then this book is for you. In this book, you will find the essentials to learning How to Analyze People. This book introduces readers on human behavior and body language, the in's and out, the various processes and steps involved in it.

Who this Book is for

This book contains information on how to learn How to Analyze People from a beginner level.

Readers who can benefit the most from the book include:

- Professionals who would like to know more body language and use this knowledge to help them on their career goals.

- Readers interested on succeeding in dating situations and learn the nonverbal cues of their dates in order to respond effectively.

- Readers curious to know more about human behavior in order to help them improve their relationship with others.

How this Book is Organized

This book is organized into three parts. The parts are best read in chronological order. Once you become familiar with all the steps outlined in the book, you can go directly to the techniques which apply to your current situation the best.

The three parts of the book are:

Part One outlines the essential topics on How to Analyze People, and then learning how to apply the techniques. The section also talks about how important it is to learn these topics as a beginner in order to form a solid foundation in doing the right steps on how to read people – from introductory concepts to understanding nonverbal cues effectively.

Part Two is about How to Analyze People in more detail. You'll learn how to read someone's mind, figure out what they mean through their facial expressions, and analyzing the words that they say.

Part Three discusses more in-depth topics on How to Analyze People such as:

- Understanding someone better in dating situations
- How to know if someone is lying to you or not
- How to understand nonverbal communication on detecting danger in advance.

Introduction

If you had one of three wishes, it would probably to have unlimited strength, read other's minds and be invisible or be able to fly. These are the main choices that people make when such social media quizzes arise or if they were given hypotheticals by friends.

Reading minds is always one of the top five if not three of people's wish list. That is an indication of how much value people place into seeing into each other's minds. Some would want it for personal gain. If you are able to read other people's minds, you can tell when they are distracted or vulnerable, and so you would have the keys to manipulating them whenever you please.

Imagine walking the streets and knowing everyone's deepest secret despite how much they may try to hide. You would instantly know how and when to leverage such knowledge to your advantage. Of course, this is not what is being advocated by this book, but it is a thought which is unavoidable.

Unfortunately, this book is not there to give you magical skills to being psychic. The book instead uses a scientific and psychological approach to analysis, which can help you analyze intention when you need to. A lot of the time, you might find yourself in a situation where you would have to read another person to assess intention so that you do not place yourself in a precarious intention.

It could be a business deal or a typical social interaction where you have to trust a stranger with your person or belongings as can happen in everyday life. A short but accurate assessment can save you from serious damage, or it can put you at ease knowing that you made the right call. The tenets addressed in this book include how to analyze people by facial expression, wording and these can be used when detecting deception or dating situations. Social considerations here include telling if your friends really mean the best for you or whether they have ulterior motives for being around you. Sometimes, our judgment is clouded because not everyone has the intuition to detect bad or good intention, so these tale-tell signs as gas-lighting or mood orientation and other behavior serves as a map towards showing what is healthy in a relationship and what is not.

The other chapters also consider the behavior models and personality analysis of people. During the initial days of psychological research on what the individual was made of mentally and what motivated him, there were several names that stood out. These included Carl Jung, Aristotle, Maslow, and Sigmund Freud. Not only did some of these personalities come up with a full analysis of the way people develop when they have little resources to when they are satisfied, they also came up with theories of why people relate to each other in the manner that they do. For example, conditioning was introduced as a typical response that individuals may have to stimuli. That is when you expect someone to do something for you, you can first teach them to do it by first doing something for them. This was the first introductions to what we know as manipulation and is practiced in different relationships everywhere.

Personality types are also an important consideration as it has allowed the classification of individuals into groups that can be easily deciphered. These were brought to bear by the Myers-Briggs model that shows whether a person is suited for this or that.

It has now become a standard by which people are judged not only for social interaction but when interviewing for career options. The analysis of people has thus come a long way and is currently actionable not only in the dating scenario for the sake of knowing who to avoid and who to take seriously but also in the career scenario so that you know how to best handle your workmates and superiors in a satisfactory way so that you allow yourself the chance to advance through the ranks.

This book will give you the tools to become well informed with person-to-person interaction and allows you the right defense capabilities from parties that not always have your best interest at heart.

Chapter 1: How to Analyze People Effectively: Getting Started

Chapter 1: How to Analyze People Effectively: Getting Started

1.1

Reading people has always been an effective skill socially and has evolved over the course of time to include different aspects of the human psyche, which are now treated as relevant cues. For example, the analysis of people previously depended on how they responded to queries but research over the past century has shown that words only account for seven percent of the way people communicate. Apparently, body language is more than fifty percent, and voice intonation represents the remaining 30 percent. This chapter focuses on what to consider when analyzing people as an introduction to the book and the background to personality analysis to ascertain the development of this science over the course of time.

1.2

An introduction to this subject would be significant to provide a context as to how the science has grown over the years. It will also be effective to demonstrate how the science affects different disciplines that have come to value personality analysis to make operations more efficient.

Even in the work environment, human resources was created to oversee the welfare of workers, but a big part of this is considering the personality type of workers that would be most suitable for that particular work environment.

1.3

The history of personality psychology can be traced to ancient Greece. Since the fourth century, philosophers have been trying to elaborate on the essence of people. It was in the year 370 BCE that Hippocrates proposed two temperaments, which were hot and cold, and these led to the known four humors that were variations of these qualities. The hot and dry combination became yellow bile. Hot and wet became blood; while cold and wet was phlegm. Cold and dry became black bile. The grouped mode of thought concerning personality was everywhere in ancient thought on the subject. Plato came up with four groupings that were intuitive, reasoning, artistic, and sensible. Aristotle was also one of the foremost to come up with hypotheses between the physical elements of the body and related behavior. It was not until the eighteenth century that Franz, Gall came up with phrenology that was a pseudoscience relating correlations between areas in the brain and particular functions.

This was some of the first work that moved away from philosophical explanations of behavior and the personality that was rooted in anatomy. At this time, behavioral linkage to mental function had not yet developed fully. Sigmund Freud and his conceptualizations of the personality were published in the text relating to the Edo and the Id. He claimed the human psyche consisted of portions, which were the ego, superego, and the id. The id was thought to control the innate behavior or the primitive instincts and desires. It represents the dark and inaccessible subconscious, which contains every inherited trait.

The ego was posited to be the bridge between the id and reality. Its task was to find realistic ways of achieving what the id wants and find justification and rationalization for these desires. The superego became the organized component of the psyche and is the moral component of the psyche.it is the center for the conscience and regulation of what drives the id and the ego by coming up with a sense of right and wrong. Carl Jung, on the other hand, added to the classification of human personality by stating people fell into different dichotomous categories that were the introvert and extrovert groupings.

Trends related to the investigation of the personality puzzle from the angle of what the underlying motivations are for the common individual proceeded during the 40s and the 50s. Not many are unfamiliar with Abraham Maslow and his hierarchy of needs. These are from the bottom of the pyramid that is the structural requirements all the way to the desires of the individual in the society and what they would be willing to do to get these things. However, this reasoning leads to a chicken and egg situation concerning what influences the motivations of people to do something and influence behavior by influencing personality, as Maslow had believed.

However, the fact personality simultaneously influences the way that a person acts depends on the motivations themselves. Overall, there seems to be no right answer as to the direction the circle flows. The puzzle that untangles the connection between personality and behavior persists when it comes to modern psychological conversations and inspires research across different fields of study.

In the twentieth century, the increased growth of analyzing people became known as psychology and led to increased interest concerning individual personalities. Apart from significant figures like Freud and Maslow,

Katherine Briggs and her daughter came up with the Myers Briggs model.

They believed knowing personality preferences would assist women who entered the workforce during the Second World War to choose places of employment that were the most comfortable and effective. The theory considers Jung's theory and asks queries that do not necessarily evaluate people according to their moral standpoint but behavioral tendency such as being extroversive or introversive.

However, the different models that have been described seem to be based according to behavior, and so they skip the part about motive. They go as deep as the requirements and the desires of the person that influences behavior though they do not attain what creates these needs and wants. Behavior according to Hartman is only the outward illustration of what is occurring within the person. The behavior-based models just identify the things that individuals do.

At the time that a child is born, for example, the first thing that people usually search for to make sure everything about them is normal is ten fingers and toes. The interesting thing is what is critical to their life experience lies in their innate personality. Personality affects all elements of the present lives particularly relationships more than physical features. It is critical for one to be acquainted with them at the least so they can align congruently with natural preferences. It provides a creative edge when it comes to emotional intelligence and success in life. Looking at someone else's driving core motive as opposed to their behavior solely provides an accurate starting point through they can be understood.

As claimed, the behavior usually does not reflect what is beneath the surface all of the time. To understand the reason why someone may be experiencing an emotion such as fear or anger, you would need to get back to their driving core motive along with their needs and wants. These are the basics as to understanding and analyzing people in general.

Some find it to be unsettling that personality is only organized in four groups within the color code. The color code though does not randomly heap individuals into the categories assigned. It only identifies the elements that motivate them. Any color thus can do any task. However, there are certain fields that enhance the strengths of each color and take advantage of talents. Those who are in red, for example, may excel in leadership positions while the ones in blue do well in the areas that concern working with others, so they are team players.

The history of analyzing people has lent crucial information to the field of psychology through the centuries. Even archetypes that were used in the first centuries are still mentioned today like choleric and melancholy. However, the accumulation of research has led the subject matter away from just the behavior itself to ascertain the needs and wants of the person in terms of their intrinsic motivations.

Your Quick Start Action Step:

1. Set up a table of your needs and preferences numbering five.
2. Write down what you believe are your intrinsic behavioral components.
3. What would you classify yourself according to melancholy, choleric, sanguine, phlegm or introversive/ extrovert?

Chapter 2: Analyzing Human Behavior

Chapter 2: Analyzing Human Behavior

Source: http://dmml.asu.edu/beams/2015/

The human race is continuously engaging in trying to fulfill their mental desires and bodily requirements within changing surroundings. The structures responsible for these cognitive processes have evolved towards the optimization of results for the bodily-based behaviors. According to scientific research, human behavior relates to a complex interplay of components, which are emotions, cognition, and action. The best way to analyze the manner in which people behave is to analyze these three components and the manner in which they relate to each other.

2.1

Human behavior is the basic denominator as to the way that people relate to the environment and to each other. It is the basic behind societal structures, crime, altruism, and social institutions. Thus, getting to analyze human behavior is a building block toward getting to know the way that people think. It also provides an insight into the motivations that drive people. This chapter delves into the basic components of human behavior to decipher the building blocks of behavior and how it relates to motivations and interactions further.

2.2

An action denotes most of what can be either observed in a visual manner or evaluated by psychological sensors. Consider an action as an initiation or transition from one state to the other. For example, a TSA official at an airport may say, 'proceed' which is to mean go on with the screening process. Behavioral actions can take place on different time scales ranging from muscular activation to activity of sweat glands, or sleep.

Now when it comes to emotion, usually this brief conscious experience can be attributed to intense cognitive activity and a feeling that is not characterized by knowledge or through logical deduction. It is usually there on a scale from the positive to the negative or unpleasant. Some of the other aspects of physiology that indicate emotion or such process would include an increased respiration rate that is caused by arousal or an increased heartbeat. These are not visible in the same way as cognition and not observed. They may be inferred indirectly through tracking of the facial expressions or monitoring arousal through the ECG.

As such, cognition describes the mental images and thoughts that a person may have and they can be verbal or not. For example, you may say, 'I'd be curious to see what that tastes like. "All of these are considered as verbal cognition. On the other hand, imagining the way one's house is going to look like after the remodeling is not a verbal cognition, it is nonverbal. Cognitions entail knowledge and skills such as knowing the way to utilize tools in a meaningful manner.

Cognition, actions, and emotions do not especially run independently of each other as their interaction allows the individual to take stock of the world around them, listen to their wishes, and then respond in an appropriate manner to individuals within the environment. On the other hand, it is not easy to tell the cause and effect for seeing a familiar face and that it may cause a burst of emotion along with a realization that is cognition so the action is equal to emotion and cognition. In other scenarios, the sequence for cause and effect can be reversed.

Considering one may be sad and thinking about a sad event like the death of a relative, they may need to go for a long road trip. That would be the action. So the emotion which is the grief and the cognition; going for a road trip; adds up to the action. Now people tend to be active consumers of sensory impressions. One may actively move their bodies to achieve the right cognitive objectives and wants or to get into positive emotional scenarios. As such, though emotion and cognition may not be directly observed, they drive the execution for the purposes of observable action—for example, when moving the body to achieve cognitive goals and desires or to get into negative and positive emotional states.

Cognition is also particular to time and situation. New information that an individual experiences is merged and adapted into the present cognitive mindset. That would allow the individual to adapt flexibly and predict the way that events in the current surrounding could be affected by actions. When the individual decides to do an action, you can achieve the decision in a timely setting. In other light, the cognitive system has to manage the interplay that would exist between flexibility and stability. The former is significant as one would some several responses to stimuli that are dependent according to the instructions and the intentions. That would then allow the individual to respond to the same stimulus in unlimited ways.

Stability though is essential when it comes to maintaining stimulus-response links that allow the individual to respond in a consistent manner to similar stimuli.

The abstract cognitions as well can be defined as body-based. The thought of limb movements, for example, can trigger similar areas of the brain that happen to be involved when it comes to the execution of movements. At the time that one rehearses material in the working memory, then similar brain structures that are usually utilized for speech production and perception are activated. When talking concerning behavior, the goal is to ascertain the way that it is acquired.

Learning assists in denoting some of the processes of the acquisition of skills along with knowledge, attitudes and the relevant evaluations and social rules. At the present, it is not a query pertaining to either/ or. There is too much evidence concerning the effect of nature and nurture alike as behavior is meant to be established through the interplay of similar factors. The main frameworks also show the role of the agent when it comes to getting new skills and knowledge. You would be able to alter the way you are through continuous skill learning during your life, and this may have an effect up to a neurological level. There are several means of human behavior settings that are still in operation at the present.

Classical conditioning for one is a way of learning where the stimulus pairing to response is analyzed. For example, the image of a beautiful woman may cause arousal. In the case of tasty food, the smell and the sight may stimulate the mouth to produce saliva in preparation. Now in the event that the food is consistently preceded by a stimulus such as a pinch on the arm or an advertisement then a new response to the stimulus is learned. The pinch or the ad becomes the conditioned stimulus and within a period can become strong enough so that it triggers the salivation even when the food has not yet been seen.

There is another form of conditioning that is known as operant conditioning, and it was first coined by B.F Skinner. Skinner had the perception that it was not necessary for one to consider the internal motivation and thought-process for one to explain behavior. In fact, he claimed to take only the observable and external causes of human behavior to be considered. His opinion was actions that come before the desirable effects have the most potential to be repeated, though the ones that come after the undesirable effects have a lesser likelihood of being repeated. As such, operant conditioning would rely on a premise that behavior that can be followed through by reinforcement is going to be reinforced and the likelihood is that it is going to happen again during the future.

There is such a thing known as positive-reinforcement, which happens when the behavior rewards the frequency of the stated behavior. In addition, punishment happens when the behavior is followed by a stimulus that is averse and causes a decrease in that particular behavior. A negative reinforcement though is when the behavior is followed by a removal concerning the aversive stimuli.

Now, these learning theories provide a form of guidance in the knowledge of information about the population as individuals and as a group. The manner in which the human being learns is appraised on an emotional and physiological basis. That may have effects on the way that people act and behave in the future, as people tend to attend to the way that it makes us feel. Now behavior may be attained through learning, irrespective of whether the actor implements an action or does not do a certain thing depends on the linked incentives and risks. However, the question is what factors are motivating the decision making process. The theories like the social learning theory allow for a base set of attributes.

Human behavior and decision-making happen are affected by emotions even in the subtle ways that are not always recognized at first. After going through with an emotionally fueled decision, the tendency is that people may proceed in the imperfect reasoning which is driving it. As such, a mild incidental emotion when it comes to decision making can last for a longer time as compared to the emotional experience. One example of the manipulation of the state of mind affecting decision-making had been done by researchers who had the desire to know how willingness concerning assistance could be impacted by positive emotion.

In the study of the research, there was a coin that was placed in a phone booth, and it was placed in wait for passersby. Actors that were working for the researcher came in and wanted to make a critical phone call. The participants of the study that had found the coin were much happier, and so they allowed the intruder to make a phone call, while the ones who did not find the coin were not affected at first, so they were more likely to reject the requests of the actor.

The research that has been done on human behavior concerns the way and why of people's actions. Though it has already been established that human behavior can actually be complex as it is easily influenced and shaped by several factors that a lot of the time are not recognized by the person. That is to say, there are overt and covert behaviors that come from the conscious and subconscious areas of the mind. Consciousness details a state of awareness that is for internal thoughts and proper perception of information coming from a person's surroundings.

There is a large part of behavior that is actually guided by unconscious modes. The human mind in this way can be related to an iceberg in that there is a lot of information but not all of it is visible to the naked eye. Overt behavior tends to describe any of the elements of behavior that are observed such as the body movements or other actions. Similarly, physiological processes like facial expressions like blushing and the dilation of pupils may not be obvious, as one would have to strain to observe them adequately. Subtle changes in the processes taking place in the body may be hidden to the eyes of the observer.

Rational behavior may be considered as actions that are impacted by logic. There is also irrational behavior that illustrates actions that are not objective or logical.

The patients that are suffering from forms of phobias illustrate a part of irrational behavior. For example, you may have a phobia of snakes or spiders. The tiniest rustle of fabric across your legs or neck may make you immediately believe there is a snake that is on your person even though there is no such thing.

These examples of contrasting behavior types show the extent to which behavior is complex and how it is influenced within the human psyche.

Your Quick Start Action Step:

1. Start a self-analysis chart according to conscious and unconscious behavior.
2. Which behaviors do you have that fall into these groupings?
3. Create a hundred-word summary

of your personality type from the results.

Chapter 3: Evaluating the Different Personality Types

Chapter 3: Evaluating the Different Personality Types

3.1

Personalities are grouped according to traits which are allegedly enduring attributes which impact behavior in a number of situations. The traits of personality may be friendliness, conscientiousness, helpfulness, and honesty may be significant as they assist in elaborating on consistencies in the way that a person may behave. The most popular way for quantitative assessment of traits is done through personality tests where people provide a self-report on their attributes. The psychologists have come to investigate several hundred traits with the use of the self-report approach, and this research finds a number of personality attributes that have a say as to the behavior type of the individual.

3.2

The personality evaluation through a means of testing allows for evaluation on a quantitative level as to the true nature of the individual.

It allows a means of separation from people that may behave in a similar manner in some scenarios but do not agree in other contexts. It also allows for an analysis of motivations through the results of personality type analyses. It is then possible to gauge the driving force behind decision making for the majority of people if it is possible to group them behind several labels as the label already has a framework that is attached which details reasoning and the potential for success and failure in different fields. The other thing is personality evaluation provides for behavior prediction. Now that individuals can be grouped according to already established archetypes, it is then possible to prescribe their activities and their best positions within the workforce or in a social setting. It may also be used for security reasons. Profilers in law enforcement frequently use personality assessment methods to sift potential criminals from a lineup to assess whether someone may commit a crime or already has done so.

3.3

Objective tests

This psychological test considers the attributes of the person in a manner that is not necessarily impacted via the beliefs of the examiner. That way they can claim to be indeed independent of the bias that may arise. The objective test may mean the administration of a survey that is marked and then compared against scoring frameworks that have been standardized. The objective tests can add more validity as compared to the projective tests that will be described later on. On the other hand, they could be subject to the ability and preference of the one being examined to be truthful and open about themselves to give an accurate representation. The most common set of the objective testing framework when it comes to personality psychology would be the self-reporting measure. Self-reporting protocols tend to depend on the information provided by the ones who are participating concerning themselves of the beliefs they have via a question and answer type of setting. There are several methods for testing though each would need the interviewees to give information concerning their personalities.

These can use a multiple-choice survey set up with Likert scales that range from strong agreement to strong disagreement. The objective measures include the following:

Minnesota Multiphasic Personality Inventory

The Minnesota Multiphasic Personality Inventory happens to be one of the most widely used assessment tests for clinical and nonclinical scenarios. It was first ratified in 1943 and has 504 questions, updated to 567 in 1989; whose answers are either true or false. It is mostly used though for diagnosing personality disorders as it was first based on a sample of Minnesota farmers and mental patients hence the name. The test takes between one and two hours to complete, and the responses are meant to create a clinical profile that has 10 scales. These are psychopathic deviance, hysteria, paranoia, psychasthenia, schizophrenia, social introversion, masculinity/ femininity, depression, hypochondriasis, and hypomania. There is also a scale that considers the risk factors for alcoholism. The test was once again revised in 2008 to use more advanced methods thus reducing the number of questions to 338. It may have originally been engineered to screen for psychological disorders, but with the revisions and advancements, it is slowly being used for other aspects of social life such as occupational compatibility and even relationships.

Myers-Briggs

Source: https://www.intellectualtakeout.org/blog/myers-briggs-test-pretty-fun

The Myers-Briggs personality indicator as earlier mentioned was created in Carl

Jung's theory of personality. It has faced criticism though because of its lack of statistical validity and low amount of reliability. The MBTI measures the individuals across four bi-polar standards. These include the perceiving function, which is sensing and intuition. That would measure if a person understands and interprets new information with their senses. The attitudes function entails introversion vs. extraversion which measures whether someone tends to be action oriented or derives pleasure from being alone or introspective.

Then there are the lifestyle preferences, which consider judging, or perception elements. This evaluates if the individual relates to the outside world mainly with the judging function or with the function of perception. Finally, the thinking or feeling functions measure if one tends to make a decision based according to rational thought or through empathetic feeling. Each of these functions is dichotomous, so the assumption is one is either one or the other.

Projective measures

These are sensitive to the beliefs of the examiner rather than the self-assessment of the individual.

The projective evaluations are done on Freudian theories and try to unearth the unconscious perceptions using ambiguous stimuli to reveal the inner elements of the person's personality. The benefit of this approach is it would expose particular elements of the personality that are allegedly impossible to assess through means of objective tests. For example, they can reveal the unconscious personality attributes. However, there is not a lot of validity considering there is no scientific basis for the results and they rely on the judgment of the expert analyst. For many years, the traditional projective tests have been utilized within the cross-cultural personality assessments. However, it was found that test bias actually reduced the utilization. It is hard to evaluate the lifestyles and personalities of divergent groups utilizing personality instruments according to data from a particular culture.

As such, it can be significant to come up with personality assessments that also consider things such as race, level of acculturation and the language. The projective measures include the Rorschach test and thematic apperception measure.

Thematic Apperception Test

This test has 30 cards that show what most would call ambiguous figures. The test takers are then asked to form an opinion about each picture such as the background that led to the thoughts, feelings, and the story of the characters. Like the Rorschach test, the results would indicate the personality attributes and emotional functioning. As such, the TAT that comes with open-ended storytelling and standardization is not there which makes it quite unverifiable. The Rorschach test, which is more known, consists of ten inkblots that were initiated by Herman Rorschach. In the test, those who participate are shown inkblots and then are asked what each of them looks like. The test administrator can ask questions about the responses like which portion of the inkblot is linked to which response. The test then can be used to evaluate the personality attributes of the individual not to mention their emotional functioning.

One of the problems with personality evaluations is the individuals may have a tendency to endorse vague generalization. That is why horoscopes are still popular because of their lack of verification. You can derive what you want from a particular horoscope as percent of the time it will mention some aspect of your life that you are going through and even then, you will have to fill in most of the blanks. Bertram Forer provides a personality inventory to the students where he gave each of them a unique profile. He then asked them to rate how well the profile given applied to them. What they were not aware of was that they had each gotten the same profile though they were not meant to communicate on the answers of course.

The profiles though had generalized descriptions of scenarios that anyone could be going through. The students went on to claim that the profile was very successful in describing them accurately. There was yet another study in which students were issued a personality inventory, and they were issued two personality profiles. One was accurate and based on the results of the inventory they had taken, and the other was a generalized inventory that could have applied to any individual. In this scenario, more than half of the students selected the profile that was generalized as their own. The fact is both of the studies show the way personality measures can give vague analyses of the individual and yet be accepted as the gospel truth. This impact is now referred to as the Forer effect.

As such, a key issue with using personality tests especially within the work environment is the potential they initiate for illegal forms of discrimination against particular groups. A big criticism when it comes to personality tests is they can be based on narrow samples because some demographics are over-represented. They may also skew the results of the tests toward this identity. That is to say that they may normalize one identity but at the same time sideline the others. The Minnesota Multiphasic Personality Inventory test was expanded to counter the bias as the critics argued groups such as Asian Americans, Hispanics, and the undereducated were not represented as much as white male Americans.

As mentioned, tests such as these are used often when it comes to singling out mental disorders. When used to evaluate the potential workers within the work environment though, the equal employment opportunity commission may be interrupting to them as a chance by the employer to get knowledge concerning a medical condition before being given employment. This becomes a form of bias and illegal criteria on which to base decisions relating to hiring an individual. The other issue when it comes to personality tests in the work environment is they create false negative results. Here the honest people may end up being labeled as the dishonest category, and the dishonest may become labeled as the honest variety.

Privacy issues have also had the chance of coming up when the ones applying for the position now have to reveal private thoughts and feelings when they respond. The personality tests are a great tool for learning the individual's potential within the work environment and can detect the potential for problems early on before the situation presents itself. That being said, the personality tests have also created an atmosphere that allows for discrimination and bias based on the test results. The grouping may also be used in the wrong manner if the results are handled by inept managers.

Your Quick Start Action Step:

1. Open the Myers-Briggs online page, look for the test, and answer the questions.
2. Self-assess if the results give a reasonable illustration of your personality.
3. Have a counselor give you a

Rorschach test and give you an analysis based on your answers.
4. Compare the results with the ones for the Myers-Briggs test.

Chapter 4: How to Analyze People Quickly

Chapter 4: How to Analyze People Quickly

4.1

The ability to read people quickly is one of the most valuable skill sets in the business world. Everyone you interact with on daily basis sends signals, and if you already know what to look for, each individual will unwittingly tell you how to analyze them within a short period. Everyone goes through the same human needs such as the desire for recognition, regimentation, and relationship with some holding a higher dominance as compared to others. Depending on the weight that is given to each of the needs, individuals can differ significantly when it comes to personality.

4.2

Getting to read people within the first few moments of meeting them presents an edge that could assist with confidence and handling situations to your benefit. The truth is several business deals could be made successful through knowing the motivations of the other party and short-circuiting all else to get to the bottom line and reach a mutually satisfying result. These are skills that are hard to come by, and the majority of people with them tend to rise quite quickly in their profession. So these tools can be used for career advancement and welfare. On a social point, these can also be used to separate those who have good intentions toward you and those who have ill intent.

If people were able to do this early on,

many toxic relationships could be avoided so this may be a tool you can use to limit the time wasted on relationships that are not beneficial.

4.3

When it comes to analyzing people the fact is the answers are always there. As people, we are always communicating with each other using body language, word choice, intonation, and gestures even though we do not know it. You have to know what to look for and understand what particular gestures mean to solve the puzzle. On the other hand, it is important to note these tips provided are not the surefire way of telling what the person is thinking, but they do provide an 80 percent probability as to where their thoughts are or their opinion on a particular matter.

The first thing to do is get a baseline reading so that you can be able to separate the personal quirks from the person's real tells. Now a seemingly innocent question to the individual such as how they are doing that day could be a trial to gauge the baseline as it sets up for inquiries that are more intrusive.

The next thing is to search for inconsistencies between the baseline and the gestures of the person and their words. This will allow you to form an opinion on the way the individuals express themselves. Those with inconsistencies may likely have a problem being honest. Therefore, when you have a chance to ask questions, the best approach is to be pointed concerning the subject matter. Vague questions or the ones that are open-ended usually do not work because if that person rambles, then it becomes hard to detect deception when they are talking about the matter. If you ask a question that needs a direct answer, then it would place them in a corner, and they would have to provide a straight answer. If they do not, then it is a sign of course that things are not all they seem with the person. The key as well is to be calm and non-intrusive.

After asking the questions, just observe the responses of the person without interrupting. That way, they do not have an excuse to claim they are being interrogated because if there is any escalation, then it will be from their side and come off as defensiveness. The choice of words that a person ascribes to also gives an insight concerning what the person means. For example, the term 'another,' used in conversation conveys the notion there were previous occurrences as to the subject matter. These are just terms that people sometimes use unconsciously when speaking to make their statements make sense.

Unbeknownst to them, they are providing hints as to the real occurrences when they use such terms. It may also be a clue as to their personality. Say the person used this term in a conversation about the awards they have won. That means they want to ensure that others know they have won at least one other award in the same field. This could be a person that requires the affirmation or others to reinforce their level of self-esteem. Observers can exploit this vulnerability of the person through appealing to their ego and then manipulate them to do what they want, as they are now vulnerable.

You also need to consider the personality of the individual in question. It may help to notice and observe some of the individual qualities that were first considered when you were looking for the baseline. This is to determine who they are as people and what is most important to them.

You can look for clues concerning the personality of an individual through paying close attention to the verbiage and attributes. A person that prefers to be the one directing or the dominant one can have a very firm handshake. While the ones who are happy go lucky and prefer humor will often insert a form of sarcasm into the conversation. They will make it seem like they are unapproachable sometimes because of their comments but a lot of the time, they are actually the ones who like interaction the most.

You also need to look for the hot-button issues that the person may be sensitive to. There are topics everyone is sensitive to which may intensify their emotions to create anger, excitement, or even sadness. As such, it is crucial to establish a personal bond to get to know what they consider important.

This includes questions of what triggers

emotion in them as to what their comfort zones are. This entails having a listening approach as they are sometimes not that easy to spot and you may lose someone within the first few minutes if you start talking about key issues in politics, the military, or society. The thing is to keep the preplanned conversation, and so you should enter the conversation as a discussion. Ask an open-ended question about the issue that you have an interest in. That would allow the person to share their strengths and issues concerning the topic itself.

You may also decide to share personal stories about what you have done with others concerning the same issues. A lot of the time, it may make people comfortable, and they are more likely to share their perceptions on the same issues. From that point, it would then be easier to draw conclusions about the person on particular issues. They now fall into categories such as conservative, liberal, democratic, republican, or even contrarian.

You need to consider the nonverbal behavior as well because this provides for a large percentage of communication. Body language and posture provide key clues as to the mood and state of the individual that you are trying to analyze and give information they would not provide when talking. If the person is learning in during the conversation, then it is an indication they are engaged in the talk.

If they back up, look downwards or turn away then they may not be paying attention to what you are talking about or not find any interest in the subject matter. The tone of voice may also provide some clues as to where the person is in the conversation. For example, if the person is answering or proceeding with the debate in a sort of monotone, then they are probably not attached to your concept and are not interested. In the event that they look at you when speaking and move closer, it means they are drawn to the conversation and are unconsciously moving toward the value they find in it.

It works for the inverse as well as they are likely to move from people that they do not find value in. Facial expressions are also key to analysis in the nonverbal sector.

If the person has an expressionless face

when you are talking but light up when they start to talk, then it could be indicative they find no value in what you are saying but only care about their opinion on the matter. If they nod or shake their head when you talk, it is a good sign of engagement and straightforwardness as they are not afraid to show their opinion on what you are talking about.

Emotion can become etched on the faces of people. Deep frown lines can suggest over-thinking or worry in the person. Pursed lips are a sign of negative emotion such as anger, contempt, or resentment so that could be a signal to deter from the current subject. A clenched jaw and grinding the teeth can be signs of tension, and so this is a signal to make the person more at ease with the situation.

Physical movements are also key in the analysis of the other person. We have already considered leaning and distance. The position of their hands may also be a factor. The crossed arms and legs suggest anger, defensiveness, or self-defense. That is to imply the person is not comfortable with the situation or unconsciously feels like they have to defend themselves. When the person crosses their legs to point the toes of the top leg to the person, it is an indication they are quite at ease with that person and the conversation itself.

Hand position is a factor as well. When people place their hands in their laps, pockets or behind their back, it shows they are not being straightforward about the issue being discussed. Lip biting or chewing of nails is a means of stress relief apparently. So if you are talking to someone, and they are doing this, then it is a means of easing the tension they are feeling at the time, and it would be advisable to make them more comfortable by changing the subject to something they may be at ease with or offering them a better seating position or location.

Overall, the best way to analyze the person you are interacting with is to change the approach from conversation to observance. That means retain as much as possible by being a good listener.

Now, this may be harder if the interaction is not face-to-face and over telecommunication means. However, there are still obvious signs as an engaged or passionate voice of the individual.

It is also easy to note when the person is frustrated or agitated. Their tone may change, or you may hear a sigh. It is important for one to develop a good ear to pick up these cues when relating to another person over telecommunication means because the cues become even more subtle.

When relating to someone face to face, your subconscious notices things relating to their posture or facial expression to give a summary analysis that we call gut instinct. This is harder to do when it is over text or a phone call. As such, you ought to rally for face-to-face interactions when you want to make a quick, accurate assessment of a person. That way you will have as many analyses advantages at your disposal as possible.

Your Quick Start Action Step:

1. Engage a subject that you would like to analyze over the phone, or through text. Record their answers and come up with evaluations.
2. Recruit someone else to engage the same person face-to-face and have them draw conclusions on a five-minute interaction.
3. Compare the results of both interactions and see if they

match.

Chapter 5: Reading Someone's Mind like a Pro

Chapter 5: Reading Someone's Mind like a Pro

5.1

The reason anyone can learn to read minds is that people do it on different levels already. Even though assumptions are usually wrong, this does not allude that the process of mind reading fails. People are actually able to mirror thoughts and feelings they interact with. However, individuals often focus on the reaction according to what they perceive they are going to do as opposed to what they are saying they are going to do. You usually see the body language and facial expressions of someone and correctly guess that they are sick, angry, or even satisfied. This chapter provides tips on how to assess people like you were in their head thus creating an avenue to make strong bonds with people.

5.2

Reading a person's mind entails a fair amount of focus and concentration on the person themselves. People would be impressed in the social and business sphere by how much one knows concerning the individual. This may help when it comes to building rapport because it allows them to perceive that you may assist them in solving problems. These problems may range from the typical work issues to relationship problems or whether they ought to make a complete lifestyle change, but inevitably, it would be about change.

However tempting it would be to offer advice it is not a good idea. Instead, your role would be to guide the subject to reach their decisions.

5.3

One should take a few moments to see the one who is sitting near you or you are interacting with. Take a mental snap of their facial features, hair and posture as well as, body language and all of the other admissible details. You also should concentrate on the environment that surrounds the individual. You have to initiate a mental column that distinguishes the traits of the individual and the other things that are not part of the individual. You then separate the person from the wall behind them or the chair they sit in. these objects have to be visualized within a particular manner in such a way that you would perceive the energy that is being produced.

People like talking about themselves and during this time, they relate a lot of information to you as the assessor. This includes where they have been on holiday and where they are from not to mention the names of family members. These things are mentioned in passing, and your job would be to pay attention. What you would need to do is remember the facts, do not immediately draw attention to what they just said. You can change the subject and start talking about something else. Then wait for a few minutes up to the point that they forget what they told you. It is at this time that you may mention the event of scenario with different words or phrases from that which was used by the person. The idea, in this case, is to echo the facts with different language so you create the illusion that you may have noticed it.

There is a technique as well which is known as covering all possibilities. It focuses on two of the opposing qualities. For one the positive and the negative attributes are then highlighted. You can stick to generalities as opposed to using quantifiable facts. An example, in this case, would be, 'you seem approachable but liable to defend yourself if you get harassed.'

This attribute may relate to just about anyone. The individual may accept it because it appeals to their ego. To soften the edge of the negative trait, it helps by making it seem justifiable. In the example shown, who would not be nasty to anyone who first provoked them. It makes the person comfortable admitting to being combative.

On the other hand, the aforementioned traits are a means of tricking the individual into perceiving that you have an inside track in the way they think or their personality. These should only be used as an in case of emergency scenario.

The basis of reading people is in the method of assessment and the resources that you marshal to make the evaluation. You need to return focus to the face of the individual. You may look at them in the eyes for 15 seconds. There is no need to stare at them for too long for fear of interrupting the energy by making the individual feel uncomfortable. After that period, you can look away. At this point, you may create a mental image of their face and their eyes. The question is what their energy feels like. Sit and considers as you let the thoughts and feelings of that individual fill your mind. This is the beginnings of the mind reading process so to speak.

The next step is to begin the conversation with the subject, as this is where you are liable to uncover the thoughts and feelings of that individual. You may decide on any topic you like. Consider their home life or even the career. Thoughts that will come into your mind could be quite similar to the ones that are passing through the mind of the other person. You may immediately be able to tell the person what you perceive they are thinking. If you have a great memory, then it may be possible to store these thoughts for a later time to sum up the entire impression concerning their thoughts in during the particular sessions. The key here is to appreciate and encourage any thoughts that enter your mind at this juncture. Even when the thoughts may be troublesome or dark, you may want to give the individual an accurate reading. When doing this, it is imperative that one keeps their mind open to all possibilities.

It could be that you do not have any clue that your friend is depressed and the revelation is hurting. It would be best though for your friend to know that you are on the same wavelength and know that he is suffering. The aspect of letting their thoughts and feelings come into your consciousness may seem like hocus pocus or an instruction to the metaphysical means of reading minds, but it is more natural than you would think. The act of clearing your mind and focusing on the individual clears your mind of all processes taking place at the moment, which is the first step when it comes to meditation. The subject then should fill your consciousness in that you need to take them in with all of your senses. The eyes, ears, nose and if possible touch. The brain has many untapped potentials when it comes to analysis, and we usually utilize only one or two senses to draw a cognitive map of the issue at hand. It is possible that the more senses working on the problem, the more accurate the solution will be. The fact is that the information drawn in by the senses into a clear map of the brain allows the brain to draw on higher cognitive functions and that may entail sensing thoughts and emotions. There are several other things that you may utilize to add to these tips. Upon the increase of your ability to focus on the thoughts and feelings of the subject in question, you can use other things to give you a better picture of what is going on in the minds of others.

For one there is emotional intelligence. In the event that you know the subject, you may ask if they are having similar emotions as what you are having. Sometimes, letting people in allows their emotions to pass on to you, and this is empathy though some have higher abilities to do this as compared to others. You may need to be patient here as not a lot of people are good at accurately describing the emotions they are going through or want to do in the first place. They may feel anger or frustration, and that may prompt them to close themselves off from the interaction.

It is an intrusive process as well so they may feel nervous or sensitive on the subject especially when they are ready to move on to something else. In the event the person you talk to decides to agree with the emotions that you sense, you can go on to ask if they can ascertain any reasons as to why they may be having these emotions.

In conclusion, you can start providing advice on what they need to do next when intensifying or decreasing these feelings. They would be appreciative of the foresight you are giving and recognize it as good advice. This may sound a bit like psychology as compared to being psychic but the scientific basis of mind reading is based on knowing how the mind works and so psychiatry is a crucial element to mind reading.

You also need to develop keen listening skills as when individual talks, it is important that you be in the moment with them. You should not listen just for the sake of being able to respond. You ought to listen to the other individual in which case you can process and understand everything that comes from their mouth. On the hand, you have to also listen to what they may not be saying which means reading between the lines. If the individual is not looking forward to the rest of the day, that is an indication they are quite sad or depressed, and there is a reason for this. Keen listening skills will assist with uncovering of reasons that would make them known to that individual. To succeed, there is a need to learn to listen more than you talk.

Listening is the way you learn more about the subject and their emotions which is a gateway to how they think. The reason most people may lack empathy at the present is they choose to ignore the emotional cues of others and over time become oblivious to them. We also live in a system that would make us ignore our feelings and impulses so that we can be civilized and get the work done in the right way and put a brave face through all of it. The longer that people ignore their emotions, the more they develop apathy to the rest of the world. Instead of thinking about the new email from a boss or what one may have for dinner later, you might consider how you are feeling. Professional psychics even say the more that you can respond to your feelings, the more that one would be able to read and respond to the feelings and thoughts of other people in their lives. As such, reading minds is something that anyone can do and is not something restricted solely to mentalists and psychic readers.

You may not experience a lot of success at first, but it is possible to get a lot of progress with practice. There are other considerations as well from the physiological point of view that will assist in drawing conclusions about the state of mind of the subject. For example, pupil constriction and squinting is an unconscious reaction to the situation from the subject which is to illustrate they are uncomfortable with what is going on. Other self-defensive measures include stroking the neck nodes by women to indicate they are uncomfortable, or in the case of men which is an unconscious effort to lower the heart rate. These are telltale physical signs that show observance of the body movements is just as important in reading the mind of the subject as looking at them or hearing what they have to say.

You should not ever use newfound abilities when it comes to reading minds to gain an advantage over people, as this would be unethical. If you find that you are increasingly gaining the ability to read the minds of others well, then there will obviously be the temptation to use this to get your way. Mind readers can be great support systems and friends.

Your Quick Start Action Step:

1. Get a few friends and ask them to participate in an exercise in which you try to read what they are thinking or what they are feeling.
2. Clear your mind of all distractions and thoughts as your friends start to think about something and write it down.
3. Observe them for at least a minute or so and consider everything about them.
4. Formulate what you perceive they are feeling and relay that information to them. Then

compare the results with what they were actually thinking about if they had previously written it down.

Chapter 6: Reading People through Facial Expressions

Chapter 6: Reading People through Facial Expressions

6.1

The human face is a rich source of visual information. You can be able to read many things from the facial expression of an individual. Apart from the facial expressions that are seen every day in particular circumstances, emotions also tend to manifest themselves in ways that are known as micro-expressions or ME. An ME is usually brief and involuntary as is shown on people's faces as a reaction to a fast-unfolding situation. The basis of this chapter is to include the micro expression analysis into how to analyze the way people think or what they are feeling at the moment as the two are intrinsically linked. It is also to supplement the facial analysis to the other senses when they are used as collective sites for information about the subject. If you only listen to what the person is saying and ignore the facial expressions of the individual, then this is the same as knowing only one side of the story. A lot of the time, you may find the words are not matching the emotions, and the facial expression might betray what the individual is feeling at the time. the value when it comes to understanding facial expressions is gathering information concerning the present emotions of the person, and this would lead to guiding the interaction between you and the subject accordingly. If the subject seems to be disinterested, it could be that she is just tired and it may be time to end the conversation.

6.2

Knowing the way to read and interpret facial expressions is one of the most significant parts of understanding the nonverbal type of behavior and reading of individuals. Now, most people tend to try to hide the way they are feeling through concealing it on their face. This is because the majority of interactions where this would be needed is face to face but there are instances where a conversation may be uncomfortable to the subject, or some information may come to light, and so they have to behave as though the information does not have a bearing on them while their mind is rapidly processing the effects and what they have to do. In such scenarios, the face makes telltale twitches that alert as to the way the subject is leaning and so this could alert you as the interrogator on what they are thinking about concerning the issue. This is especially helpful in situations such as interrogation during criminal investigations. It is also quite useful in social and workplace interactions so as not to be blindsided.

6.3

Facial expressions are the outer manifestations that illustrate internal changes that are happening in the mind. Identification of an expression is quite easy considering it entails corresponding muscular changes in a certain region of the face. Decoding the expression as posed by the subject in this scenario could mean either that the subject is not aware of something or the person is denying something. The expression could also be dependent according to the context. The mind has the incoherent ability to respond to a stimulus without beforehand conditioning. That is to say, it intuitively tries to come up with a logical behavior concerning the behavior of the person through association of the expressions of the subject without particular meaning. In this case, the meaning that is attained through an expression may not be the right one. For example, during a social event or at a party when one member of a couple does something that is socially awkward, the other may get angry.

However, being in a social gathering that partner may not outwardly show their anger and cover it with a smile.

That smile may allude that the partner is tickled, or it is funny to them, but this could not be further from the truth. It thus concludes that the face has a multi-signal system. The face can blend two emotions, as a person may be surprised and have fear at the same time. It is not necessary to have only a trace concerning a particular emotion on the person's face though. Words may also deceive people, but the facial expressions can be dead giveaways of showing the true intentions. There are times that the expressions on a person's face are deliberately made to communicate information though. According to Paul Ekman, the comprehensive facial expression scoring technique known as Facial action coding systems recognizes each expression within a collection of thousands of expressions that are grouped into three categories. These would include macro-expressions, micro-expressions, and subtle expressions.

Usually, macro expressions can last between three-quarters of a second to 2 seconds which is the same as 24 to 60 frames. They include the six universal emotions, which are sadness, fear, anger, surprise, disgust, and happiness. Spatially speaking, they may happen over multiple or even single sections to the face as depending on the expressions themselves. For example, the surprise expressions may generally initiate motion around the mouth, cheeks, eyes, and forehead, though the expression for fear is usually concentrated around the eyes.

By definition, the micro expressions show emotions that individuals may not want others to know concerning the way they are feeling. At times, the person that is displaying the micro expression may not know that the emotion is actually leaking out. That may be due to the fact the micro expression does not last for a very long time, in fact, micro expressions can be as short as a third of a second and so it may sometimes need electronic equipment to catch these expressions during a video interview.

Apparently, micro expressions can be classified according to the manner that each expression is modified into three types. In type 1 neutralized expressions, the genuine expression is suppressed, and the face remains neutral. In type 2, which simulated expressions the micro expression, is not accompanied by genuine expressions of the emotion and situation.

The last is type 3 for masked expressions. Here the genuine expression is completely shadowed by a false expression.

Micro-expressions are involuntary by nature, and they reveal the true emotions thus holding valuable information for the scenarios that range from the security interviews and questionings to media analysis of celebrities and politicians. They happen in different regions of the face that lasts only a fraction of a second and are universal across cultures. In contrast to the macro-expressions such as smiles and frowns, the micro-expressions are very subtle and almost impossible to fake. Considering the microexpressions may reveal emotions that people can hide, recognition of the microexpressions can aid forensics and mission capabilities by providing clues to intercept and predict situations that could be dangerous. The following is a description of the micro-expressions and what to look for when evaluating emotion.

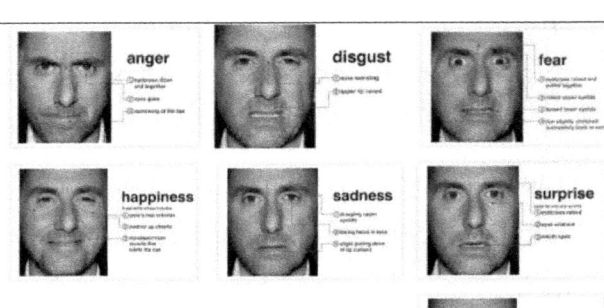

Source: http://www.subliminalhacking.net/2010/07/19/its-the-little-things-micro-expressions/

Disgust micro expression

Here you may find that the upper lip is raised, and so is the lower lip. They may not be parted, but in many cases, they are. The bridge of the nose also forms a small definable wrinkle. The cheeks are also raised in a form of query, but that is an automatic reaction. There are also two lines that show between the eyes of the subject or above the eyes.

Fear micro expression

The brow is raised and drawn together in a flat line. This is because the jaw may clamp shut. The wrinkles in the forehead appear in the center between the brows and now across. The upper eye has white showing but not the lower white. The upper part of the eyelid may also be raised, though the lower lid is tense and drawn up. The mouth draws open, and the lips can be tensed or stretched and drawn back.

Surprise micro expression

The skin below the brow can be stretched, and the brows can be raised and curved. There are horizontal wrinkles that form across the forehead. The eyelids are usually opened to the maximum, and the white of the eyes is shown both above and below for the individual. The jaw may also draw open and the teeth can part though there is no tension or stretching in the mouth's muscles.

Anger micro expression

In this case, there are vertical lines that appear between the brows of the person. The lower lid of the eye can be tensed, and there is a long eye stare or focus as if the eye is bulging. There is tension in the lips as they may be pursed together when the person is trying to hide their emotion or the jaw may be clenched together. The nostrils may be dilated as well, and the lower jaw can jut out.

Sadness micro expression

The lower lip may pout outwards, and the jaw comes up. The corners of the lips are slightly drawn downwards in the opposite direction as with the happiness micro expression. The inner corners for the eyebrows are also drawn in and then upwards. The skin below the eyebrow may triangulate with the corner going upwards.

Hate or contempt micro expression

The side of the mouth may rise. Eyebrows may stay level, and the lips are pursed together. There are no creases, but the eyes may constrict ever so slightly.

Happiness micro expression

The corners of the lip are drawn

backward and up. A wrinkle can run from the nose to the outer lip. The cheeks go upwards and the lower lid can show wrinkles or can be tense. There are crow's feet near the outside of the eyes. The mouth may be parted or not as the teeth can be exposed or not.

The most significant assessment tool when it comes to assessing facial expressions is to know when someone is not being straightforward. Lies become obvious especially when you learn to read cues at the time of a conversation. From what we have gathered, micro expressions show the tiny muscles governing the eyes, eyebrows, and cheeks respond to different emotions felt. There are other means other than micro expressions than reveal if the individual is avoiding telling the truth on a particular issue though. The eyes for one provide a link to memory and imagination. However, imagination is good; when it comes to weeding out the lie, imagination is not the best possible thing. For example, when an individual looks upward and to the left when asked a question, it is usually because they are recalling information or utilizing the memory. That would illustrate the truth. However, when someone looks up and to the right, they are probably using their imagination to fabricate information and this is something that works well with lying.

The eyebrows are also key areas that represent honesty in the individual. When a person lies, they tend to raise the eyebrows in a subconscious attempt to show they have nothing to hide when they in fact do. They may also blink a lot and hold their eyes closed for a longer time. All of this is an unconscious attempt by the person to buy time for the subject to see which path the story needs to take, so they do not have inconsistencies. Similarly, the person may avoid eye contact or force it if they feel that it is necessary. Generally, eyebrows have been known to show emotional cues other than deceit.

For example, lowered and knit together eyebrows can show anger, and when it is not to cover a truth, a raised, and arched eyebrow shows surprise. Inner eyebrows that are drawn up show sadness. If a person is not truthful, and they are caught in the lie, they may react by being untruthful. Apparently, nervousness may cause a rise in temperature, which causes blood to flow to the extremities and to the face, which then causes the person to blush. This phenomenon may happen because of other stimuli, but it should reveal uneasiness in a person.

Smiles are also key towards reading facial expressions. That is because people often fake smiles when they do not want others to know what they may be feeling. It could be to mask fear, surprise, or anger. Now a fake smile does not have an effect on the eyes. The fake smiles are mostly accompanied with what would be termed as 'dead' eyes. A real smile though comes with eyes that are lit up and constricted. This is because more muscles are utilized in happiness than with the forced demands.

Speech is the other element of facial expression. It may be contentious as to the role it plays in facial expressions, but the fact is it can be useful for learning about the other forms of facial language. In this case, when speaking, liars can repeat themselves, as it seems they may be trying to convince themselves concerning the lies that they tell. A lot of the time, they may speak quickly to get the lies in a consistent piece. When talking, inauthentic individuals may have an increase in their heart rate as they are a bit nervous about their statements and wonder if their statements will be believable. In the event, the individual they are talking to is familiar with reading facial expressions and other indicators concerning deception then they would probably be found out very soon. They may also be defensive and answer a question with a question or just play the victim in that case.

Not only do the facial expressions come with an illustration of the authenticity of what the person says but the body language also does a good job of showing discomfort. Sweating, fidgeting, and an increased heart rate as mentioned reveal that the person may be lying or at least not being straightforward with the entire truth.

It could take some time to catch these indicators, but at the time you master the ability, you will get to know the direction of the truth from very early on, which is a valuable trade secret for one to have.

Your Quick Start Action Step:

1. Select two close friends and engage in them in normal conversation about things you know about them to be true.
2. This sets the baseline for tells then observe how they move their face and eyes.
3. Ask them to lie to you about any subject and mark down tells.
4. Try to assess how many things you caught them lying about.

Chapter 7: Analyzing People through the Words They Say

Chapter 7: Analyzing People through the Words They Say

7.1

The manner in which an individual uses their words shows a great deal of information about themselves and their audiences not to mention the current situations they could be in at the time. The choice of words from individuals may provide hints concerning their motivations, social status, age, and gender. We are able to sense if the speaker is emotionally distant or close to the subject if they are introverted or extroverted. The basis of this chapter is to consider the potential ways of analyzing the subject by the way that they talk. The chapter will consider the history of this analysis from the Freudian concepts to the present analytics that involve technology. Since the advent of the text message, people have become more prone to communicate over email and text than face-to-face. In so doing this analysis ought to adapt and consider this as a factor in analyses as it is important to consider all aspects of how talking has evolved and how it affects reading what people are thinking at the time.

7.2

Now, you may question why it is important to assess people from what they say if it is already possible to develop a good idea from just looking at them or being around their space. The fact is an analysis is needed to analyze a person's thought process.

That would mean using all the assets that you have at your disposal including the auditory functions of hearing what the person has to say. As indicated previously there are many benefits to getting to analyze a person quickly. It can present an advantage when you hear cues and relate them to particular personalities, and this would be very useful in high stakes situations. It can help during competitive games or during the work scenario such as interviews and panel appraisals.

7.3

People may change the way they talk depending on the situation. For example, they may feel a bit self-conscious if it is a recorded interview, but there are still going to be shifted in the speech style when the circumstances or the mood changes in a significant manner. This can be similar to the way that bilinguals change languages when they are in the middle of speaking to someone. If a foreigner is asking for directions in a country and someone overhears the conversation who knows that foreigners language, they may interject and help give the foreigner directions. Now, that foreigner will immediately become relaxed in their speaking because there is a form of familiarity they gain when they address this second person in their native tongue. It is a natural reaction, as people tend to speak their second language in a more formal tone than they would their first one.

Further, then that, the words that are written or spoken are an expression of personalities and inner thoughts. Though beyond the meaningful content when it comes to language, there are many insights into the mind of the author that are hidden when it comes to the style of the text. The manner that the author expresses thoughts and opinions shows character. At the time that people may present themselves in a particular manner, they may try to select what they perceive to be appropriate nouns and verbs but they are not likely to have a control on the pronouns and articles.

These are some of the words that initiate the styling of the text and it could be less subject to being manipulated by the subject in this scenario.

There is a program known as the LIWC

or the Linguistic Inquiry Word Count program that was used for examination of speech characteristics and tallying nouns and verbs in different groups to expose the patterns in the speech of public figures that would have otherwise gone unnoticed. The software evaluates the number of times a speaker uses words in particular groups like emotion, perception, and words that show some of the complex cognitive processes. It also tallies the function words like numerals and conjunctions. In each of the big groups are subsets. These ask questions if there are more mentions of sad emotions or happy ones. LIWC answers these queries and the psychologists would then have to ascertain what the numbers mean.

There are political candidates that

illustrated differences in speaking approaches. John McCain was one of the candidates who spoke in a direct manner and directly to his constituency. This vocabulary was also very loaded with emotion, and it was impulsive. Obama in contrast usually makes many causal relations that indicated complex thought processes following deductive considerations. On the other hand, he tended to be vaguer as compared to his Republican rival. The skeptics pertaining to the usefulness of LIWC have illustrated that a number of these attributes pertaining to Obama and McCain in the way they address people could be considered without the use of a computer program.

The comparison between the two candidates has also illustrated how many pronouns were able to show for particular terrorists. Between the years 2004 and 2006, the number of times that Al-Zawahiri utilized the pronoun 'I' tripled but it was consistent in the case of Osama Bin Laden. Usually, the higher rates of I words are there to correspond with feelings of threat, defensiveness, and insecurity. A closer inspection of the 'I' use in context may tend to confirm this matter.

The personality of an individual can be ascertained just by looking at the way that they text. It is also possible to make accurate judgments concerning an author's judgment just by reading through their article. Word choice can predict as to whether an individual is depressed, suicidal or is being deceptive on the subject matter. The interesting thing to note is that swearing can also make the person appear to be persuasive when they text or talk. The word choice of a person may tend to alter when they are lying though. According to an analysis that was done of over 200 transcripts liars produced more words that were based according to sense, and they utilized a fewer number of self-oriented type of pronouns when they were lying than when saying the truth. The things that happen to be easier for the brain to process on average seem to feel truer as compared to concepts that are harder to process. Therefore, you may find that people who instill extra steps when they are texting or complicate the explanation are more likely than not lying. This is one of the reasons that people like the familiar more than what is not. It is also the reason why people go for the simplest explanations as compared to the more complex but accurate answer to the problem.

Now word choices like 'I' can be quite telling about the situation. Those who are less powerful say it the most as individuals use 'I' rarely when lying to distance themselves from the matter. In the same sentence though, 'we' can be quite strong. Just through saying it can make individuals feel more positive to you and it can initiate a feeling that relates to familiarity. The couples that say 'we' a lot of the time when describing the state of their relationships usually can be satisfied. The use of the word 'you' can be a bad sign. As such, we words may end up saving one's life. In a project, the patients that had heart failure were interviewed by spouses. In this survey, they were asked questions such as, how they coped with heart conditions that one of them was suffering from and what they think aided the most in their conditions. The more that the spouses used we-words in their answers, the more healthy the patients were at a later time. Thus, words that illustrate partnership like 'we' are indicative of people that are satisfied.

The statistical study of language though is a bit young, and it is clear that analyzing patterns concerning the use of words and the writing style may lead to insights that would have remained hidden otherwise. Considering these tools come with predictions according to probability. The bottom line though is the way that we write and speak can reveal a lot about identity. The following describes a sampling of the variables that can be detected using style-related words including articles and pronouns. When it comes to age, as people get older, they may refer to themselves less and less and use emotions that are related more to positive emotion and fewer emotion words. There is also use of more future tense verbs and less past tense verbiage. Public figures and poets that have been published are more likely to utilize the first person singular pronouns at the time they are depressed, or they become suicidal which indicates a lot of absorption in themselves. When it comes to gender, the women may also tend to utilize pronouns and references to other individuals. The men have the higher potential of utilizing the prepositions, big words, and articles. Finally, when it comes to trauma, during the days and weeks after cultural upheaval, individuals are less likely to use 'I.' They instead revert to 'we' as a means of a social binding effect.

Your Quick Start Action Step:

1. Get your phone and look for a text thread on a matter that you know to be the truth.
2. Get the same person you were texting with, bring them in on the experiment, and ask them to try and deliberately lie to you about something while trying to cover the fact they are so it seems like the truth.
3. Note their text patterns.

4. Meet face-to-face with them and have them try to do the same in person and note their word choices.

Chapter 8: Analyzing Someone on Dating Situations

Chapter 8: Analyzing Someone on Dating Situations

Source: https://www.psychicscoop.com/10-huge-red-flags-to-avoid-in-dating/

8.1

Romantic attraction happens to be one of the biggest mysteries of social interaction among people. People love 'connection' on different levels and some of it biologically geared to ensure the continuation of the species. That being said, there are several aspects that go into connecting with another person. For example, 'Do they have similar likes and dislikes? Are they responsible? What motivations do they have for being with me? And so forth.

Most people would love to have the ability to read minds if only for this purpose so they could sift through individuals that have the wrong motives toward relating to them and find the 'one' quickly enough. The purpose of this chapter is to give tips during the dating phase that will allow you as an individual to read between the lines and have a better chance of not ending up wasting time with the wrong individual.

8.2

Reading your date has purely social benefits for the individual but would work for a better living on the overall. This way, you can have the peace of mind that comes when you are sure of someone that you have a romantic connection with. The dating phase comes with a lot of uncertainty precisely because the world is quite diverse and social attitudes to romantic connections are increasingly changing. That being said, motivations now vary from the benign to the malicious where people are concerned. It would be nice to know that you at least have an edge when it comes to being a judge of character than have to rely on the judgment of others to verify one's choices in a mate.

8.3

Body language is an especially effective means of deciphering the intentions of a person that you are dating because it says more than their words could within a short span of time and it gives a hint as to where their interests really lie. There is a theory that implies that when people get 'butterflies,' it then causes the capillaries in their face to swell up and that in turn makes their face to develop itching. If your date tends to scratch their face a bit more often than they normally would around their friends, then it is a sign that they are interested in you.

If the person is also holding up their hands to their face, it may be a sign of shyness or nerves that would be linked to having a crush. People who feel vulnerable may touch their face with their fingers apparently so this is a good sign. It is also in their eyes. Cartoons have previously hinted at this body language facet by showing love interested through beating hearts in the eyes of someone that is attracted to someone they just met. In real life, it is all in the pupils of the person.

The pupils tend to dilate when they look at something that the person is attracted to, and they shrink when they look away. People also tend to use their subconscious expression to assist in opening the eyes when they perceive what they see. If a person raises their brows slightly when you are talking that is a clear indication that they are interested in what you have to say. This is why people say the eyes light up when someone is around their partner because the pupil gets bigger and their eyebrows are raised to open the eyes farther. The other thing is the facial expression. Facial expressions are also a factor in this matter. Though it could be obvious, checking the face of your partner is one of the best ways to tell how they feel about you. There are several people who just do not know how to ask how they feel about a certain situation, which means if your date is not interested in meeting again then it should be obvious from the way their face is oriented.

In this case, flushed cheeks, eye contact, and natural smiles are all great signs of interests. However, if they are not interested, then they may make droopy facial expressions or show micro-expressions that are related to contempt or sadness. Eye contact is another facet to pay attention. The eyes have numerously been claimed to be the windows to the soul, so if your date is maintaining eye contact with you throughout the entire duration, then it is safe to safe they have no problem with being open with you. Therefore, if you are telling a story or just talking about how the meal is, then you need to pay attention to the eyes of your date. If they are looking back at you most of the time instead of at their meal, then it is definitely a good sign.

Body posture is a factor as well. Leaning into someone is a great sign even if it is not a response to a romantic connection. When people are interested in what the other person has to say, their body unconsciously orients itself to the direction of the person because that is where the words are coming from. Have you noticed that you may sit near your best friends when you are out eating in that order? It is quite natural for people to sit close or lean close to them regardless of the situation.

The same thing applies during a date but just on a higher level. If the two of you are sitting across from each other though you still avoid leaning in to hear each other better, then not all may be well, and the ice is not being broken. This can also be related to the direction the person's feet are pointed towards. People tend to point their toes in the direction that they want to go. Therefore, if you are sitting across the table from your love interest and they have one of their feet pointed towards the door, then it could be time to call the cheque and skip on the desert because they are already through with the date mentally. Unless you have already started talking about going to another location, then the probability is that your date is thinking about going somewhere else.

In this regard, there are warning signs that you need to consider which illustrate that your date is a bad choice and could present serious issues for the relationship in the near future. These red flags may or not be related to body language but are in the way they handle their interaction with you. People may misrepresent themselves to you, however; it is hard to keep one's nature bogged down toward others even if their significant other is present. Now they may be nice to you when they are trying to impress you but are extremely rude to the wait staff and ushers or service personnel. This is an indication of how they perceive people who provide services and will be a reflection of how they will treat you further along in the relationship. It also shows that the person has a superiority complex and feels they are above others especially if they are tasked with serving them. The other red flag that an individual needs to look out for is pushing boundaries.

The boundaries themselves do not have to be sexual. The individual, in this case, may actually be sharing too much personal information too soon and this can be an instance of pushing the boundary. If your date tells you very personal things over the first cup of coffee together, then that may mean there are serious emotional issues that are happening at the time. For example, if you ask if you can buy them something to drink and then the person declines and they explain that they have had bad experiences with alcohol, then that would be very reasonable and even commendable. Though if they then go ahead to tell their deepest and darkest secrets during the small talk phase, then it could be a signal that their definition of personal boundaries is very different from that of others.

The other thing that ought to be more overt is they act irresponsibly. Now depending on their age and circumstances a date that may live with their parents might not be a red flag. There is a difference between someone that just cleared college and is trying to get their life started and a thirty-five-year-old that is still living in the basement because they do not feel like living on their own. You might also find that they engage in inappropriate social behavior as there are time and place for particular topics. If your date is a bit immature or does not recognize particular social norms on the first few dates, then it is probably going to get worse as they get comfortable. Finally, they may also not have respect for bills. This has two faces as they can brush off bills and defer it to you or others. That entails they are trying to give an image they cannot live up towards. Now, on the other hand, they may have the money, but they overspend too much. This could be a sign that they do not have respect for the resources especially if you are the type to be frugal.

Your Quick Start Action Step:

1. Go on a random date with someone that your friends vetted if you are single.
2. Go out with your partner if you are not single.
3. If it is the latter, pretend it is your first date and read cues from their body language and what they say and mentally note them on your phone.

4. Go over the summary once you are done and evaluate.

Chapter 9: How to Detect if Someone is Lying or Trying to Deceive You

Chapter 9: How to Detect if Someone is Lying or Trying to Deceive You

9.1

The fact is that we are surrounded by deception, as it is a key facet of our lives. However, it would be great to be able to tell which of the things we hear lies are and what is the actual truth. The statistics on lying illustrate the average individual hears between 10 and 200 lies every day, strangers lie at least three times during the first interactions and college students lie at least a fifth of the time they talk to their parents. These are all understandable, but it would save a lot of energy if there were cues you would follow to find these deceptions out. This chapter considers the different red flags that you need to pay attention to when interacting with someone that will scream deception.

9.2

Deception cues have been around for some time now, and they point to the way the person is interacting which is to mask their involvement in an issue or distancing themselves from particular knowledge. Getting to know these red flags will provide you with a fighting chance of uncovering lies that could cost you both financially and socially. There is no limit to how much waste you can short-circuit by implementing this knowledge.

9.3

There are tells which would explain the lack of veracity, and these may include fake smiles, blushing, blinking, flared nostrils and reduced pupil sizes. You should notice and pay attention though it does not necessarily mean a red flag. Though these may be indications, there is just too much room for false positives to go by the expressions by themselves. It can be quite hard for the trained or experienced interrogators to select the liar according to the process of facial expressions. However, this can be accompanied by other things that are then going to be identified as a red flag. As such, by itself, these facial suggestions are not an issue but if they come along with any of the following, then there ought to be a reason to worry. The next thing that one would do is to repeat the question. It may be that they are making sure that they did hear you asking them the question correctly but a lot of the time, this is a method used for buying time, or they are trying to unpack the question and ascertain how much you as the interrogator know. That would be to give you as much as they estimate you know about the situation without giving you too much information, so they give up their position entirely but also enough information so that you do not necessarily get suspicious concerning the situation.

People who lie also use unnecessary superlatives in their language or have an unqualified desire to shut the conversation down and jump to another topic. If the subject uses terms such as 'tremendous, immediately, or absolutely' there is a good chance they are deceiving you. There are instances when these terms can be appropriate, but they are the exception to the rule as people who insist on including these words in their speech could be trying to uplift their argument or they could be trying to provide a distraction to the entire process. On the other hand, they may not want to talk, or they move the conversation to another subject.

That is because the zone of deception is mostly murky and they have to create scenarios which fall into alignment so that you do not question because there will be an instance where things do not make sense. Now for someone that is not very good at lying, it could be hard to keep this up so they would prefer to move to another subject, so they do not have to keep juggling words. This is also not the best tool to tell if the person, in this case, is being untruthful but it is a start.

The subjects may also contradict themselves. In this case, the person that is talking may add details to the story that in turn contradicts them. At this point, you can catch them in the lie, though there are some who have a talent for weaving the truth and the lie in one setting so that they seem to be the same thing. The fact is many people who are truthful when asked to retell a story a number of times are going to remember additional details. It does not necessarily mean the story is going to change, but it will make more sense. In the case where the subject is trying to be deceptive, you will find that the person that is talking is not adding any new details that contradict them but instead they are going to claim to reduce the scope of things that they actually know about. They will feign not knowing about something they had earlier explained in detail. The subject may also illustrate inappropriate emotions linked to the situation. For example, they may give terrible news but have the matching emotions to boot. A grieving widow that had something to do with the death of her husband will not be able to display the sadness of his loss and vice versa adequately. There will be something that is missing from their presentation. At the same time, the emotions may flare up with someone who is being deceptive, and they may overreact unnecessarily over a trivial issue. For example, they may get overly angry, defensive or even cry when questioned, as it is a method to distract from the overall issue.

You have heard about the phrase claiming that you ought to look someone in the eyes in reference to telling if someone is lying or not. There happens to be some truth on this matter. The lack of eye contact is a nonverbal sign that the individual is lying on that matter.

The reason is that eye contact is something intimate, but there are some people who do not mind looking into your eyes while lying through their teeth. It is still possible to catch them because the body has an instinctual desire to distance itself from lies or being caught in them so you may find that the pupil tends to constrict when the person is lying. The eye movement may also slightly move up and to the left. This is toward the creative centers of the brain, which construct the script of what to say. A movement to the right and upwards is toward the memory centers which means the person is remembering the events as they happened.

Lying can also be represented by the posture of the subject. An individual that is lying is usually going to show it with their body language. They may do this by shrinking in on themselves, slumping to protect their body subconsciously while they are lying. It is a commonly accepted theory that the more an individual is going to allow their body to be open, the more likely it would be that they are being honest or trying to be honest at the least. That is because when the body is open, you are more vulnerable most of the time. In the event that you observe an individual changing their body language to calm himself or calm their body, then there is a probability that they are lying. For example, the person could fold their hands or cross their legs.

You may also focus on the way they move and the frequency therein. Lying individuals mostly want to trick the one who is interrogating them into perceiving that they are calm when they are not, and their movement may betray this fact. A lot of the time, they may keep hands at their sides and sit very still or speak in a slow manner while keeping facial movements small. That is because they are trying to fake calmness and these behaviors can be a tell that they are lying. It is not very easy to tell because the people who do this try to make themselves less significant in the conversation and could have a lot of skill in deception.

To catch these types in a lie, you would need to be very receptive as to the way they conduct actions like shaking their head. Your body can betray you a lot of the time when lying and so just a tip of the head can be what undoes you.

For example, there may be a verbal or nonverbal disconnect if an individual is saying yes though they happen to be shaking their head as to say no. this may be a potential signal of being deceptive. There may be subtle changes in behavior as well especially if you have spent some time with the person. You may notice that the person who was boisterous suddenly reduces their energy by a few notches. It may not be dead silence, but there will definitely be a change. The key, of course, is to come up with a baseline for the behavior of the person and then search for deviation from that particular baseline as a response to a stimulus. Individual deviation to something said may not necessarily mean the person is lying, though it is indicative that they are uncomfortable with the topic. It needs to be backed up with other symbols that have been outlined in the aforementioned text like body language and emotional reaction.

Your Quick Start Action Step:

1. Have a close friend tell you base truths about themselves

that you can verify to set a baseline by marking their body cues and emotional tells.
2. Have them try to lie to you about different things that are entirely up to them and mix it up with the truth.
3. Compare the results of what is the truth and what is a lie according to what you analyzed.

Chapter 10: Detecting Danger Before it is Too Late

Chapter 10: Detecting Danger – Before it is Too Late

10.1

Dangerous interactions that could lead to social, workplace, financial and even physically related harm are all around us. Most people were raised not to be too trusting of people until their motivations become apparent but someone's we become too comfortable and let our guards down. It is at this time that predators looking to take advantage to further their own interests at your expense. Now the signs of a toxic relationship are sometimes quite easy to spot because the people who are perpetrating them even on the first contact are very open about the way they treat you like there may be physical or verbal abuse. On the other hand, there could be subtle signs that something is not right concerning the relations between you and a close friend, a family member, a romantic partner or even a coworker. It does not matter what form the relationship takes, it is crucial to pay attention to how it makes one feel. This chapter is based on the ways to detect a toxic relationship through various cues to extricate yourself and prevent further damage from occurring.

10.2
Toxic relationship detection is probably the underrated benefit to the current society.

So many people are not aware they are currently within poisonous relationships that are leading nowhere and are doing them more harm than good. If it were possible to free more people from the yoke of unneeded stress in their lives, it would make millions of people much happier overall. It could also help the perpetrators to introspect and ascertain the reasons as to why they are prone to lashing out at others. Some of them truly are not aware that they cause harm in their relationships sometimes especially if it is emotional and verbal abuse because they may have grown up in such a scenario, so that is what they know. Pointing out to the problem allows one the next process to happen which is finding out potential solutions and allow for healing. In the event that the person refuses to deal with the issue, it also allows for the process of distancing oneself from the situation.

10.3

A big red flag when it comes to toxic relations is the other person is quite controlling. In this context, it may not always mean they are physically threatening or violent, but it may just mean that you are too frightened to share what you truly feel. As such, you might find that you are constantly walking on eggshells because you do not know what that person may think about you if told the truth. This normally happens during relationships when one partner is controlling or has standards that are outrageous. If you find that you cannot be yourself around them or you do not want to for fear that it will bring too much conflict, then this is an outright red flag that the relationship is toxic.

Similarly, there is gas lighting, which can happen in different scenarios apart from relationships. This happens when the other person knows very well that you are in the right during a conflict or argument, but then they do their best to confuse things and muddies the waters by then trying to cause you to doubt your reasoning and make it seem like you are off base and overreacting.

They are usually very good at manipulation, so they make it appear as if you are the one that is the aggressor and you are crossing the line or are unstable while they consciously know what they have done. A master in this practice facilitates the process is different nuanced and subtle ways, so it does not appear to be obvious in the first place. For example, you may hear the person is at a business terminal when you call them though when you meet them later, they manage to convince you that it was probably the sounds in your background that you were hearing and they were at home. In another example, a boss at the workplace may promise to give you a raise, but when you improve at work that month and approach them, they get agitated and tell you they promised it to you after a three months appraisal, so you are being impatient and unprofessional. Gas-lighters come in every form and can make a person doubt their sanity in some cases. Gas-lighting is damaging because not only is the person lying but they are also messing with the reality of the other person, and this can add an extra layer of betrayal to the whole thing which places your mental health in a place of risk. These are all matters that could force the victim to go to therapy for some time.

The other thing is that in the case of a relationship, your partner makes fun of you or reprimands you in front of other people and friends even after you have had a discussion on the issue. Public teasing in itself is not good as a sign within a relationship especially in the event that you have already made it clear that it hurts. A good partner would not try to humiliate you to make themselves look better in front of others. Even if they say that you are being oversensitive, it is clear that this is often a red flag and you may never at any one time feel emotionally safe while in the relationship. Now the other issue is mood relation. Sometimes the other party can wake up on the wrong side of the bed. This is a normal occurrence and is not any reason to be worried, but for some, it can present as the norm within the relationship. Now sometimes, the other person at work or at home can be moody or irritable because they are hungry or they have not slept. If it happens regularly, then it is a sign of emotional instability or immaturity.

Emotional indiscipline allows them to perceive they have the right to vent as they please to different individuals in their lives because they were not having a good day and they often use this as a blanket excuse when they are questioned about it. This is a red flag, as it will cause a lot of distress to the other partner including walking on eggshells and being held emotionally hostage, ultimately tampering with the mental health of the other party.

Now red flags can also be considered for online platforms because the majority of communication at the present is often held via social media or other online platforms. The first thing is to read between the lines of their dating profile, which is to consider how they communicate. Consider how they write and what their hobbies are. Ask questions about their profile picture and whether picture looks too good to be true. The interesting thing though is a majority of online users lie on their profile picture, above 80 percent to be exact. They may have taken flattering photos of themselves at their best angle while the rest would show they have dirty dwellings, or they are overweight or are older than you would think. There is some profile red flags to pay attention to such as a lot of the use of 'I' statements, which may be indicative of narcissism. They may also refer to themselves as very good looking. You also need to avoid anyone that claims they do not advocate for 'drama' or 'games.' These are things that are generally expected and so if the person announces that they are not for that type of relationship. The probability is the opposite is what is true.

You should also consider photographs that are out of focus within their profile or those which are blurry. If they form the majority of the images therein, it is a good sign they are not secure about their appearance and have something to hide. You also need to stay away from any language which can be claimed to be domineering or possessive. Anyone that uses phrases like 'I will not tolerate' or 'I cannot take a person who' and has a long list of demands is just a potential headache in waiting. Negative positioning in their language like a lot of use of words such as 'won't,' 'can't' and 'shouldn't' are signs of a person that is extremely hard to please and actually has a negative attitude.

If you decide to exchange numbers, and then they decide to spam you with several texts at a time and become overly attached before getting to know you, this is a red flag. These are the signs of extremely low self-esteem and potential paranoia as they could become very possessive. There also others that go directly to the point and engage in sexual euphemisms at once after exchanging numbers. Now depending on what you are looking for, this may or may not be appealing, but if you are not comfortable with the approach, then it should be a signal to abort the whole thing. Finally, they are those who ask for financial assistance. Granted they do not always make it so obvious nowadays as they did in the past. It may be a long con that starts in a few dates before the individual decides to finally show their hand and ask for it.

Before you give anything out, you need to analyze very carefully not the character of the person in question because that may be faked, but you need to consider how you both came to this position. Cons are very good at engineering circumstances through a series of coincidences that if considered would show that not everything is above board. Therefore, you need to consider the sequence of events and finally are at the conclusion of how you came to such a position.

Your Quick Start Action Step:
1. Write down a list of preferences you would like in a partner, work employee or a boss.
2. Evaluate dos and don'ts you can live with and those you cannot abide by.
3. Compare the results with the way things are at work and in your relationship if you are not single

or with close friends.
4. Take steps to eliminate or reduce toxic relationships from your life.

Conclusion

Thank you again for owning this book!

I hope this book was able to help you to (know the basics of getting to know people and how to adapt this to relations with others. The best place to start is to ascertain your own behavior. In the book, the first chapters concerned the analysis of human behavior, which is what makes people tick. It was found that motivations behind action were the most important thing to consider when it came to analyzing the behavior of individuals. The subject may have particular emotions, but these are not the driving forces behind their behavior, and so their motivations gain ultimate importance.

The next step is to evaluate yourself and personality. Once this is done, the next step is to evaluate the toxic relationships that you have in your life and find solutions on how to make them better if you are to blame and consider how to solve the issue if not.

You need to analyze your behavior and what drives it, and from there, your personality type can come into view. A number of personality evaluation modes have been mentioned such as the Minnesota model and Rorschach test, but the Myers Briggs seems objective enough and is versatile so that it can be used for social scenarios as well as the work environment. In this way, you can then tell whether you are an introvert or an extrovert, whether you are judging or perceptive, or use intuition versus sensing. These personality groupings make it easy to categorize you as one or the other in key facets of social life. From hence, you are able to judge which relationships you can cultivate with others and the type of people that you would most likely get along with.

You can also use the model on others and be able to judge who they are and why they act in the manner that they do. Creating understanding is the most productive thing you can do with the knowledge gathered from this text. The other tools provided include being able to analyze people in high stakes scenarios using a variety of features like their body language and their facial expressions.

Some of these cues are obvious while others are much more subtle. The tools presented in these chapters are meant to be practiced in the same way that a person would exercise to bring out their muscles.

Everyone is different, and so a cue done by person 'x' may differ from one done by person 'y.' With a sufficient amount of practice; you will be able to tell the emotional state and orientation from a short time of being in a person's presence. The benefits of this have already been covered extensively in the text. Social tools have also been covered to ascertain the red flags on dating online. Considering this facet of the society is steadily taking hold of communication outlets it is only fair the book covers how you should handle online dating and the various things to look out for. Things such as demands given too soon and suspicious looking profile photos are negative indications. These are just some of the things you need to think about.

Thank you and good luck!

www.ingramcontent.com/pod-product-compliance
Lightning Source LLC
Chambersburg PA
CBHW051545020426
42333CB00016B/2108